KOANS

MY STORY OF ANOREXIA

KOANS 公案 A paradoxical anecdote or riddle used in Zen Buddhism to demonstrate the inadequacy of logical reasoning and provoke spiritual awakening.

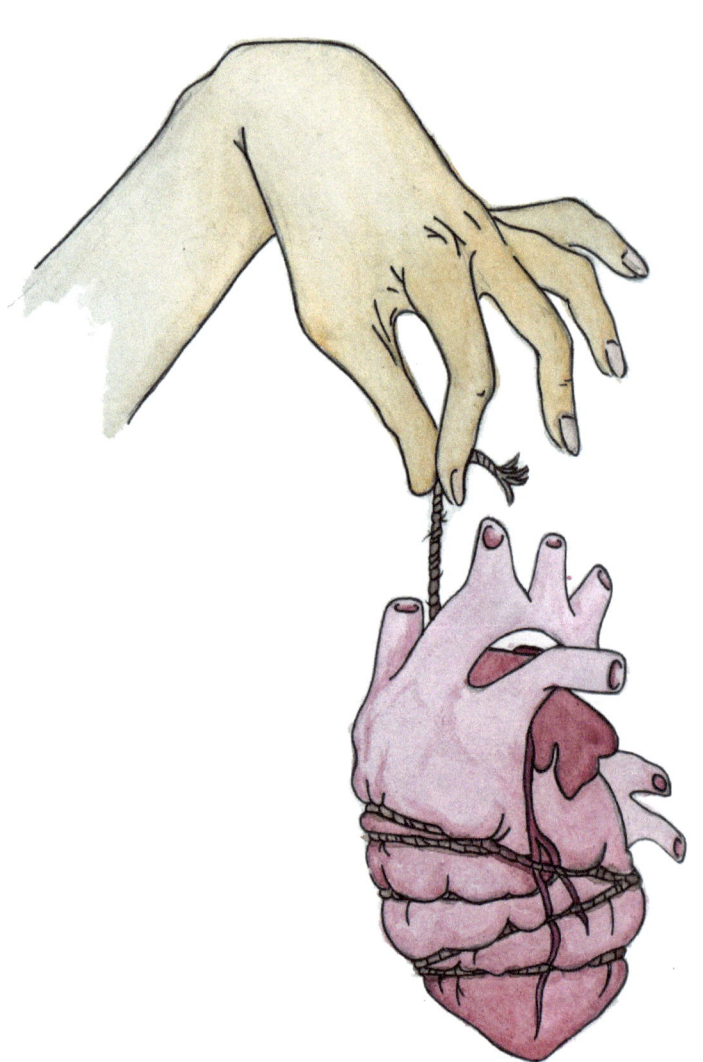

"Owning our story
can be hard but not nearly as difficult
as spending our lives running from it.
Embracing our vulnerabilities is risky but
not nearly as dangerous as giving up on
love and belonging and joy —
the experiences that make us the
most vulnerable. Only when we are brave
enough to explore the darkness will we
discover the infinite
power of our light."

- Brené Brown,
The Gifts of Imperfection

Original Cover Art, Poems, and Essay by Janet Gilmore
Illustrations by Emma Gilmore
Editing and Arrangement by Brian Gilmore
Cover Design and Page Layout by Emily Zimmerman

Copyright© 2020 by Brian Gilmore

All rights reserved. No part of this publication may be reproduced, distributed, or transmitted in any form or by any means, including photocopying, recording, or other electronic or mechanical methods, without the prior written permission of the publisher, except in the case of brief quotations embodied in critical reviews and certain other noncommercial uses permitted by copyright law.

Published by Village Books
1200 11th Street, Bellingham, WA 98225

Printed by Ingram Sparks

ISBN: 978-0-578-61094-8

With love to our mother and grandmother.

Be at peace and may your words help others find peace.

emancip-
I marri-
my bo-
He's made
play God
be wh-
I don't know
any
In doing
real
to suit an-
It pains, it
but its not
as the real

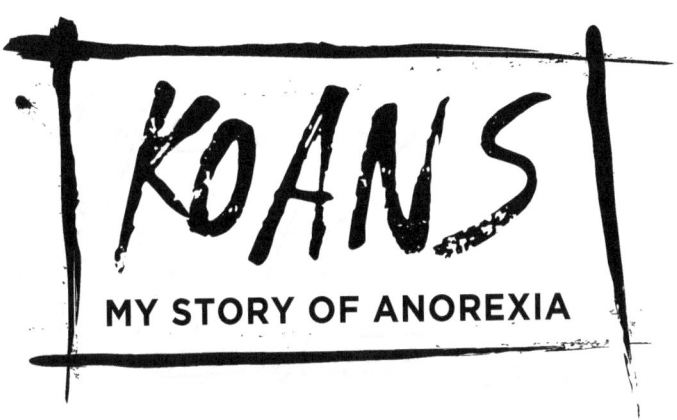

KOANS
MY STORY OF ANOREXIA

Poems & Essay by
Janet Gilmore

Illustrations by Emma Gilmore

Table Of Contents

10 Foreword by Brian Gilmore
     The World

23 Starving To Find Fulfillment
     Perception Of Reality
     Being
     Myself
     Going Home
     Wanting
     Floating
     Mood

43 How Do I Get The Pieces To Fit?
     Body Image
     Body Sensations
     Demon
     Sensations
     Invisible
     Time
     Fear To Panic
     Dawn
     Where Am I?
     Unreal

71 Am I Fading From The World?
Who Am I?
Fog In My Mind
Life And End Of Life
Looking Back

82 Afterword by Janet Gilmore

Foreword
Brian Gilmore

Not flesh of my flesh
or bone of my bone
You were not born beneath my heart
but in it

    I knew these words before I ever remember hearing them spoken to me. They were lovingly repeated to me by my mother throughout my childhood and, as an individual adopted during my infancy, they provided a deep sense of security, love and connection to my family and the world.

    My mother was a gift to my life as much as I was a gift to hers. She said that when we first met at the adoption agency, we stared at one another with a deep, powerful gaze and within seconds, I gave her a huge smile that impressed all in the room. It was a magical moment that she said confirmed our relationship as mother and child and gave meaning to the difficult journey she had endured in her attempts to have a second baby. I arrived to my home and family a week earlier than planned, on my mother's 31st birthday. The best birthday present a mother could ever receive, she told me more than once.

After giving birth to my sister Kristi in 1955, my mother had a series of miscarriages which eventually resulted in her inability to bear more children. While at first overwhelmed with feelings of loss and punishment, she finally recognized her suffering was a necessary labor and the path she needed to travel for she and I to find each other. Her loving words above, the first poem she gifted to me (likely adapted from the beautiful poem Not Flesh Of My Flesh by Fleur Conkling Heyliger) certainly affirms that one need not share DNA to truly be family.

Janet, Kristi & Brian (1963)

This story is a portrait of a life struggle painted from a collection of poems that I would receive from my mother some 25 years after her gift of that first poem that lovingly assured our bond. While I embrace our destined-to-be mother and child relationship, there was another reality that brought us together. My mother, Janet, developed an eating disorder as a teenager in the late 1940s, long before public awareness of the disease. This demon which gripped her so tightly would test and take its toll on her total being throughout her life. You might say that I was born from an eating disorder since it was the physical effect that anorexia had on my mother in her 20s that led to my adoption. I felt its controlling presence within our home and within our relationship until it finally took her life in 2002.

Janet's eating disorder deeply affected all of us who loved her. My father was overwhelmed with concern, frustration and helplessness by her stubbornness and strong will. These characteristics were amazing strengths when she set healthy goals but destructive and terrifying with her steadfast refusals to eat and some of the obsessive-compulsive behaviors that stemmed from her anorexia. I remember laying in my bed as a 6-year- old and hearing my dad pleading for my mom to just eat something and her refusals escalating to a tantrum of throwing food and dishes. I know my parents loved each other dearly and that my father, who continued to support my mother financially throughout her life after their separation in 1971, still feels the pain and guilt that he could not find a way to support her recovery. My sister, grandparents, friends, and I were all challenged in our attempts to help her break free from her disease. She experienced anorexia at a time when information, empathy and treatment were different than today. Seeing someone you love starving in front of you and thinking that they just need to eat, it's hard not to try and coax and coerce food down their throat. However, the more this was attempted, the stronger her refusals would become. My family had to trust that institutionalized care, when she hit rock bottom with her starvation, was the only course of action. Yet she pleaded that if we truly loved her, we would never put her through that hellish experience again. But every time she returned home, twenty-plus pounds heavier and with a glow of health, it was just a matter of months before she would lose the weight, and herself, to the disease again.

I was fortunate that, after my parents separated when I was in 2nd grade, my mother willed a way to "get her shit together," as she liked to say, and temporarily maintained an eating routine that allowed her to raise my sister and me as a divorced, single mother. At that point, she stood out as a free spirit and eccentric in our mostly conservative, suburban neighborhood of East Grand Rapids, Michigan. On her daily long walks with Cher, our Basset Hound, through our "Leave It to Beaver" neighborhood, she strutted her head-turning style that included big 70s moon boots, bleached jeans, silver lipstick, large African and South American jewelry and an oversized army jacket. She enrolled in college and finished her B.S. degree in Environmental Studies at Aquinas College. She also became an activist, attending various protests and writing editorials to our local paper. Janet was the hip and cool mom that I adored and my high school sister was most likely embarrassed by.

However, her will and ability to keep it together remained a struggle. Most likely what had made it possible for those few years in the 1970s was the reality that if she failed, she would lose the opportunity to raise her children. She consistently showed an abundance of unselfish love, acceptance and care for others yet struggled to love, accept and care for herself. As my sister moved out and on to college and independence and I became a teenager needing my own space, the disease, never fully gone, crept back into our home and increasingly pulled her back into despair and isolation.

It was a stroke of luck that I found my mother's book of poetry and journal essay on her struggle with anorexia. As part of her therapy in the late 1980s, Janet journaled nightly. She would fill the pages of these books with raw expressions of her state of being and yearning for peace, bring them to her therapist for private discussion and then toss them into the trash. By this time, I was living out of state and visited home only a few times a year. In 1991, she sent me a letter containing a few "mood poems" she had recently written. She told me that she had never written a poem in her life and they had just flowed from her. She selected a few to share with me, with instructions to just throw them out if they were too depressing. On a trip home not long afterwards, I happened to look inside the garbage can in the garage and there was a discarded journal titled Koans, Mood Poems that contained the entire collection of her poetry and an essay titled "My Story Of Anorexia." I put the journal safely away in a keepsake box.

Janet was four months away from her passing when she met my first child, Emma. I had quietly hoped that somehow a new grandchild could inspire a recovery from her anorexia that had almost completely consumed her. I so wanted the two of them to get to know each other and share a bit of life together. At their meeting, my mom was in such an emaciated state, weighing barely 80 pounds and a recluse in her home. However, the love in her eyes and heart shone through and amidst all her pain there was a beautiful moment between grandmother and granddaughter, with a look that can be seen in so many photos of her with her own children. Months before, when learning of my wife's pregnancy, she had said that we would have a daughter and then a baby boy—and she was right. As with so many times before, she apologized for all she had put us through with her eating disorder, said that her "nonsense" needed to stop, and vowed to get better. I had learned in my late 20s that pleading or getting mad could not exorcise the demon that held her so tightly and I remember telling her how much I loved her and thanking her for being the amazing mom that she was. It would be our last time together.

This disease or demon (as Janet often named it in her writing) devastates not only the afflicted but all who try to understand and support them. She was so much more than the disease that she fought over six decades. To me, these writings reveal the shape and form of the demon that lived in my home throughout my childhood and always lurked near and within my mother.

Because of the intensity and despair within Janet's writings, I waited until Emma was 15 before sharing them with her. To my surprise, Emma, who is an avid and talented young artist, began painting a watercolor for each of the poems as an interpretation of her grandmother's expression. It's been an amazing connection between a grandmother and granddaughter who had only met once and is the inspiration for this project. From her found poetry and writings she has left a gift of her expression, allowing a glimpse from the inside out into a lifetime battle with an eating disorder.

It is Emma's and my hope that by sharing these poems and illustrations, my mother's expression may provide some insight, empathy and understanding for those suffering from an eating disorder.

Brian Gilmore *arranged and edited this book from the collection of his mother's poetry, letters, and journal. Brian lives in Bellingham, WA with his family. He is a school counselor and filmmaker.*

*Brian & Janet
(1965)*

A Note To The Reader

Janet's story was arranged by dividing her essay, My Story Of Anorexia, into three sections and then interspersing select poems from her journal, KOANS-Mood Poems, to reflect and deepen her expression. The essay appears on the all-black pages in white font and reads continuously.

We are deeply grateful to Bellingham, WA artist and graphic designer, Emily Zimmerman, for her beautiful layout and design of Janet's writing and Emma's illustrations.

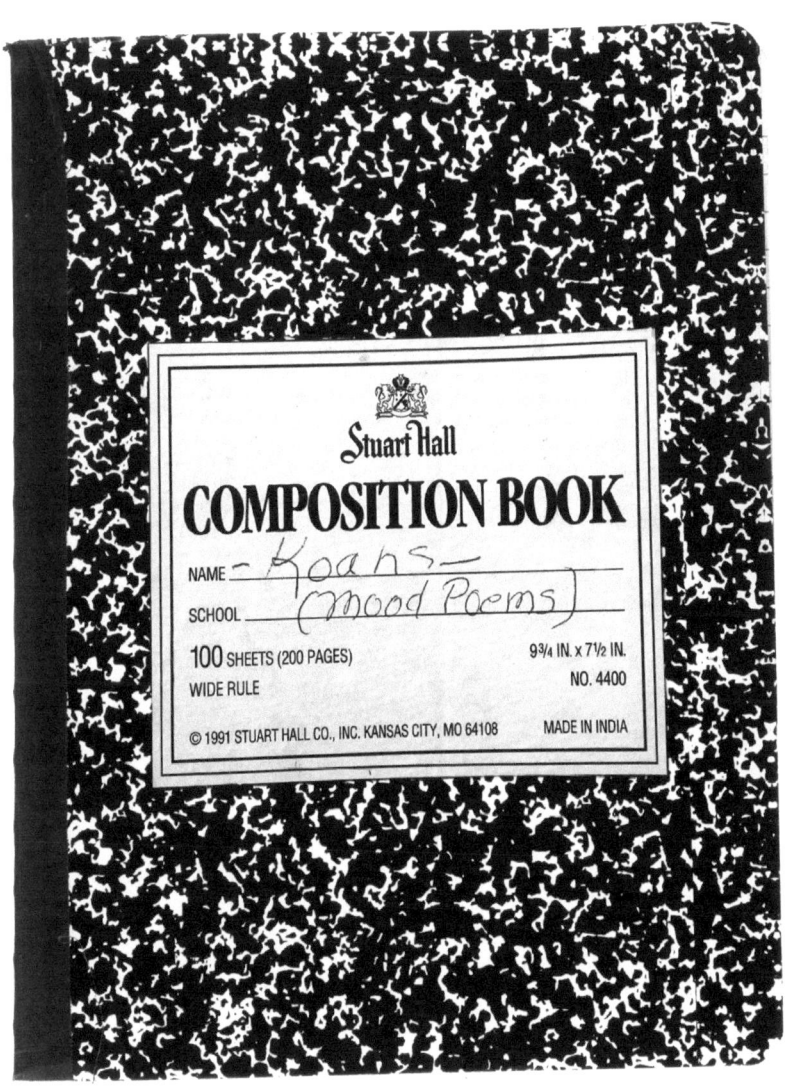

Original Journal containing Janet Gilmore's writings and poetry.

THE WORLD

It has been said that the world is round
My world is flat

I stand at the edge

Trying not to fall off

into nothingness

tho. Whe
controlling,
controlled (anymore etc
don't nee
better than
word —
3, 4, 5 x a d
they functi
a paradox
I wake
organized, bec
my day +
+ when and h
can do it. a
fail at th

STARVING TO FIND FULFILLMENT

There are two of me.
One, in control, one being
controlled by anorexia. All
the same though because when
I'm most controlling, I am
most controlled. I say to
myself, I don't need to eat.
I am better than the rest of
the world, eating three, four,
five times a day. Yet, they
function and I don't?

A paradox!

PERCEPTION OF REALITY

Your perception is not mine
Mine is not yours

Your conception, my exception.

Black is all colors
White is none

Do we see the same?
How to communicate?

We can only guess

BEING

Alone, we are unique

In society, we blend, meld and become where, not who we are.

We leave ourselves behind as we step into the world

Wear different disguises

Yet, all alike, play-acting a role,
Expected clones of each other

Back alone, we become unique again.

MYSELF

By myself, I am complete

In a crowd, I am alone

Out of place, out of space.
I rush to seek solitary peace again.
Regretting that I can't relate
Envying those gay souls who
function and enjoy.

Would that I could!

Alone, I give in to pain
and I'm not ashamed.

Alone, I can cry
and feel desperation and despair.

Outside of myself

Inside myself

Not the same!

I waken to the day, thoughts organized, a routine to follow. What to eat, when to eat, how to eat. Sometimes, I can do it. Occasionally, I fail. Then, I am full of self-loathing and I go completely out of control, gorging myself until I'm sick, convincing myself that I won't ever eat again, forever.

GOING HOME

I awake
It's morning again
A time to begin

I start my day with careful planning
Frenetic activity, familiar rituals
Desperate to keep the demons from coming
to turn me inside out and upside down.
I become then a different being,
driven by instinct- To survive?

I want to go back in time to a gentle place
Where everything fits and the demons are asleep
in my subconscious.

WANTING

Wanting all
The good
The beautiful
The comfort and joy.
Is it too much?

I go to extremes, seeking the most
The best
The perfect.

It's not a perfect world
Will I ever learn to seek the compromise?
The conformity?
The level between high and low?

It began when I was 15
and felt my lithe, boy-like
shape rounding out into that
of a woman. I didn't recognize
that it meant I was normal,
becoming an adult, but I was
frightened at what was
happening to me beyond my
control. I wanted to go
back in time, where there
were no expectations and
responsibilities. So, I dieted
my way back 20 pounds,
relishing the comments by
those who loved me that I
looked sick and too thin.
It escalated when I found a
way I could eat and still
lose weight, bulimia.
Still in control, I thought,
but of course I wasn't. It
had me! For 6 years, I felt
euphoria, superiority, ultimate
control. Then my previously
strong body began to fall apart.

FLOATING

My body floats,

Light as air

Above the below,

Beyond boundaries

Empty, but somehow fulfilled.

Why can't I maintain this serenity?

The world says,

"No!"

MOOD

Heights of ecstasy
Depths of despair.
I seek the in-between

Extremes control my mind
and action.

The feelings come,
Unannounced
and unprovoked

I cannot control,
Hard I try.
I run in circles of emotion
Not intellect

I've had twelve hospitalizations and as many doctors and psychiatrists. I gain weight, just to lose it, and myself, to anorexia again. I see this fat lady in me, trying to get out, even at 70 or 80 pounds for a 5'6" frame. I don't know how to do "it" right anymore. Three small meals a day? How can I put myself through that loss of myself so often? I'm able to handle one, then I fall into bed, exhausted. I seem to feel it's dirty, sick and wrong to eat and give in to "them." Who are "They" anyway? I call "them" the authority figures that are forcing me away from my addiction. I cling to it like a raft on the turbulent sea that's my life now.

more alone,
but never g[o]
back to ha[ve]
children le[ft]
I'm older [and]
~~together~~
my Dr.
cajolling +
into submi[ssion]
with all th[e]
in me. Wh[y]
to be sick, [want]
to others?

HOW DO I GET THE PIECES TO FIT?

BODY IMAGE

I manipulate,
twist my body to an unreal image.
I play God,
trying to be what I seek
But I don't know what it is anymore.

In doing this,
I destroy the real me
to suit an image.

It pains
It pleases
But it's not working
as the real person tries to
break the bonds I impose.

Where can I find a middle?

BODY SENSATIONS

Feelings with no reason
Out of world,
In the world
What shall it be?
Today,
Tomorrow,
Yesterday
Never the same
I seek the balance
Intense sensation
No sensation
Uncontrolled and wild

Then nothing at all.

This seesaw existence went on until my marriage of 20 years fell apart. With my kids to bring up and life's responsibilities mine alone, I temporarily willed a way of somewhat normal eating and put the illness aside.

But never truly gone, it came back to haunt me when my children left the nest.

DEMON

Demon, perched on roof.
Turning blue to grey
Light to dark
Right into wrong.

Fluttering in my chest
Like a bird.
A scare-beast
with no face.

Is he me?

Now, I'm older, yet, no respite. My doctor is my parent, cajoling and threatening me into submission. I fight with all the strength left in me. Whatever for? To be sick, to look frightening to others? To gain sympathy and attention? Still yearning back to childhood when I was carefree.
Am I seeking to find Nirvana in this constant state of "high"? A hallucination, a fantasy life, lonely and slowly being cut off or cutting myself out of the world and from those who truly care what happens to me. Shutting out the love and causing pain and anguish to them as I did long ago to my parents and my husband.

SENSATIONS

I don't see a real world
I don't feel it.
I live inside myself
with dark thoughts
and strange sensations.

My senses are distorted.
My life has turned around
What was isn't
And what is, isn't either.

What and where am I?

What has happened to the person
I thought I was.

INVISIBLE

There are many Me's
inside Me
Docile, Meek
Assertive, Angry
Capable, Helpless
Honest, Dishonest

None of them
All of them in one body,
One mind.
How do I get the pieces to fit?

Looking at my present life
is like looking through the
wrong end of a telescope.
It's becoming smaller. My
days are short, some go by and
I can't remember a thing I've
done. I hurt so. I fight so!
Sometimes I fear if I just quit
and face myself, I won't see
anything at all. Things that
used to give meaning and
substance to my life are now
brief and floating. I try to run
away, but I can't escape myself
and what I've become.

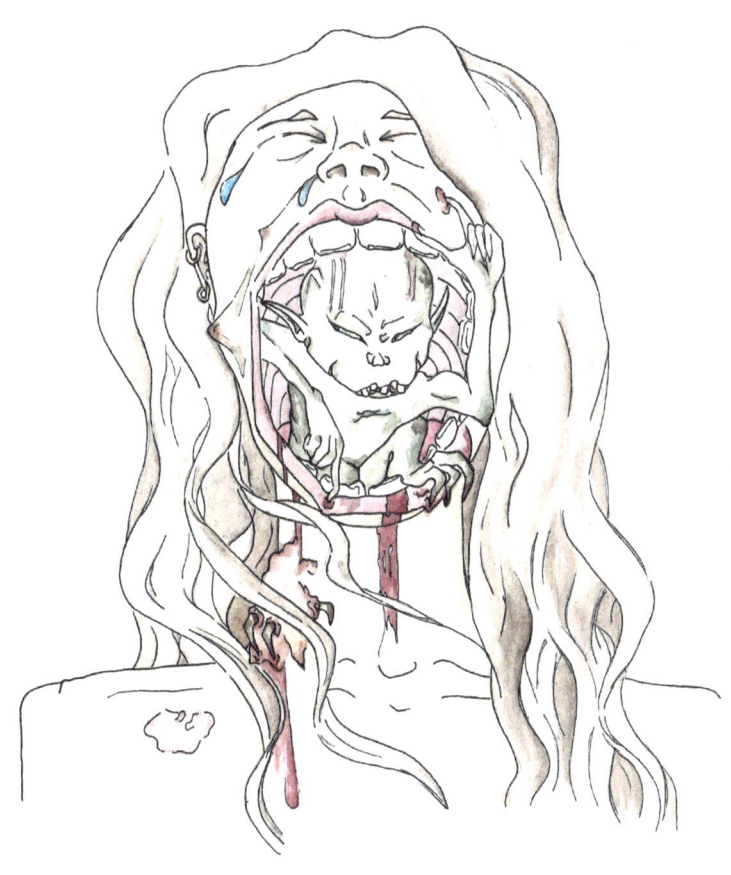

TIME

Time governs life
Time organizes,
Legislates,
Demands,
Proclaims.
We live by the time
Of day
Of night.
Days long, nights short
We can manipulate it
Change the hands of the clock
But, we cannot stop the march of
minutes, hours
Steady, on and on
Cannot slow it down
Or speed it up

Until it ends.

FEAR TO PANIC

Depression, an almighty tyrant
Leading me to desperation.
Anxiety to panic
Fear to terror

And all within my hidden unconsciousness
Suddenly comes into focus.
So clear, so unyielding
Living in my being
Unsolicited
Unwelcome

Yet,

Impossible to escape.

I am told to eat three meals a day. Small meals. I eat and feel out of control overwhelmed with fear and anxiety.
I want to be happy and healthy again, but I don't want to pay the price. In lucid times, I make connections and plans. A list for the day is a constant. More than not my list takes longer and longer to accomplish and some things don't get done at all.
I find relief in routine.
If I can have sameness and no surprises, I have a better day. I make plans according to what is expected of me. But, my needs are less, my responsibilities diminished, as others take over. Then, I rebel and stubbornly wrestle them back. Two steps forward, four steps back,
over and over.

DAWN

Day dawns, usual pain.
Oh, to welcome it with joy again.

My mind is whirling
I feel goodness in flashes.
My birds welcome the day!
Dog begs me to arise and live.
All creatures give joy I seek.

Then, back to womb
To wake again,
The same.

WHERE AM I?

The sky above,
The earth below.

Somewhere in-between, I float

Like a meteor seeking its spot
Not knowing where to belong.

    In the middle of somewhere?   Or

                    In the end of nowhere?

I am thinking of a breakthrough, a desperate need to finally recover. "Just do it!" I guess that's what's left. Yet, I'm programmed not to. I mustn't think, analyze, regret and most of all don't let self-esteem become confused with self-hatred. Yet, I always find an excuse from having to eat. Something hurts too bad, "How can I eat with sore mouth, nose, ears, nausea? It isn't what I want. I'm not hungry. It doesn't taste right." I know eating would lessen the pain but I'm very confused and not thinking straight. Why am I stuck in this place? Why am I doing this to myself? I don't have any answers to these questions. I must seek outside myself, not internally. It's time! Time to change! Time to take steps to release myself from myself. I have to rely on what others tell me. The solution is out there, not in here.

UNREAL

The unreality
Senses gone amuck
Smells, tastes, the air I breathe
Not the same
So strongly bizarre
So frightening.
I'm so scared of myself
I'm not real
Up in space, trying to get down
Am I fading from the world?

hospital. She
Another, 35¢
meals. nee
any length
My pres
me offensively
me. And I
dwell on it
scolding. I a
meals daily
eating in the d
it escalates in
then I'm sick,
for days.

AM I FADING FROM THE WORLD?

WHO AM I?

Where am I?

Who am I?

I'm lost, looking for the sea of tranquil
All I see are turbulent waters

I can never plan on never, ever, or always
Or, even hopelessness

I'm lost, and I don't know where to find me!

What is real?

What is unreal?

Is there a reality?

I know what I must do, but still can't seem to do it. Obsession, compulsions and emotions rule me. I make lists, notes on the refrigerator, then stubbornly ignore them. My doctor encourages me to eat three small meals daily, not counting the calories, not stepping on the scale and losing myself to nonfood behavior and thoughts. I try and it escalates into a binge, tearing me back to my cocoon of desperation, fear and loneliness. Then I'm sick and dieting again for days. I am very discouraged but not ready to give up. It's strange that my body keeps running at all.

FOG IN MY MIND

The fog descends
The rules no longer apply.
Disorganized, frenzied
Not knowing what or where.

The world turns

Mine stands still.

My mind is lost along the way.
The moment is!

The past and future don't count anymore
Only the moment,

The dark place where intellect disappears
Emotion and obsession overwhelms

Reality is gone, far away.
Slowly to return in remorse
and desolation.

LIFE AND END OF LIFE

Joy and sorrow
Peace and turmoil
Goals accomplished
Mere existence from day to day.

No surprises
No future
Just today, getting through.

Will I go on to a different plateau?
Or will it just end?

Hopes and dreams
All over.

Grateful for the good
Sorrow for the bad.

Is there anything left?

Just considering doing this is scaring me. I have too many excuses not to.
"My stomach is nauseous, my mouth, teeth, glands, throat hurt too much, and so on." I feel too caught up in this disease to let go and live a different lifestyle. How can I change years of habits and behaviors? I feel there is no solution; I will always be an anorexic, just as an alcoholic is alcoholic for life. The difference is that one can stop drinking, but one cannot stop eating.

Anorexia is not a diet, it's a disease. Acute anorexics don't care about the emaciation, but only about trying to reach a stage of euphoria that comes from starvation. It becomes harder and harder to eat. Meals are regulated and sparse; and only certain foods are to be eaten; not diet food necessarily. A competitive eating regimen. Occasionally, it breaks down and bulimia occurs; eating large quantities until satisfied, and then deep self-hatred and depression. Then the cycle begins again. It's a vicious circle of binging and starving; and what for?

LOOKING BACK

Regret not
Move on, a higher level
Don't look back where it is dark.
Seek the light beyond.
Strive toward renewal

Failing again

Falling again

Begin again.

Finally, Nirvana

Never to return
Someday, someway
I will find what I seek.

Afterword
Janet Gilmore

*My Experience With Anorexia:
A message to those trying to help individuals struggling with an eating disorder.*

A physiological problem manifesting in disordered eating. It usually starts with extreme dieting to get thin and small (and thus dependent and childlike). The dieting becomes distorted as opposed to normal dieting and becomes obsessive and compulsive.

At first, a great "high" is experienced. A clean feeling, a feeling of omnipotence, having control over one's body. As it progresses, the individual becomes thin, wasted and is driven to frantic exercise and more food restriction to get even thinner. It's never thin enough.

Eventually, the person becomes ill and is hospitalized, sometimes being tube fed which is very stressful, a loss of control. As soon as the patient leaves the hospital with 10 or 20 pounds added, they usually lose it again and are in need of therapy.

I went to three different eating disorder programs at mental facilities. None helped because the forced eating, the punishment and the restrictions are unbearable. I was forced into a chair and force fed. I was made to drink Ensure and if I didn't eat, bathroom and recreation privileges were taken away and I was treated like a prisoner, a disobedient child. I still found ways not to eat: hiding food, lying, taking out the food tube, etc. The food disordered person is very devious.

A nurturing which I needed was withheld. A nurturing, authoritative approach is needed. The person with an eating disorder needs care and understanding, not punishment to regain self-esteem and must be recognized as an individual, not just a thin, sick person. Force is not going to work. I was put in isolation, locked in a cell like a jail with no windows, strapped down so I could not move or exercise. Trays of food were brought in and left uneaten. I was there for 16 days and became so sick and dehydrated. I couldn't even go to the bathroom unescorted. Finally, the doctor took over and sent me to the hospital where I was cared for, fed by tube and trays, and gained my health back. I left the hospital and was OK for a short period, then lost it and was placed in another medical psych unit. There, it was even worse. I was made to eat 4000 calories a day and was so frightened of all the food I was ingesting. My brain had ceased to function normally and the forced eating nearly destroyed me. I came out feeling so out of control and feeling very bad about myself. I couldn't eat again and started the cycle all over. I lost all the weight I had gained in the hospital, 20 pounds in 6 weeks.

Then, I found a psychiatrist who was understanding and nurturing but also authoritative in his approach. Still in the grips of the disease, I now function, but, I am not truly living.

Taking what I know and have experienced, this is what I believe is the best approach to help someone who is in the grips of this powerful disease:

The individual needs an understanding, sympathetic analyst. One who can be firm, yet empathetic. Someone not just mad and putting down the individual for being sick. Anorexics can be very disruptive and aggressive. They are extremely difficult to reason with. The disease can so deeply possess them, causing them to be dishonest, conniving and manipulative.

A good nutritionist can be a vital part of the recovery helping the anorexic see how important food is to live and teaching them to eat right. Food is part of life and eating it should be a good experience. A nutritionist can reteach eating habits and reassure the patient that they will not be allowed to gain too much weight. Careful monitoring of food and calories so the weight gain isn't so frightening, especially at first. Most feeding programs just want to see a big weight gain so they feel they have accomplished a cure. But, if that happens, the patient reverts, too frightened by their changing self.

A nutritionist can support a new eating lifestyle that includes a variety of food and not enormous portions, which gives the individual a choice and the feeling that what they are eating is good for them. Lots of vegetables, fruits, grains and bread. Maybe a good dessert but careful on binge-type foods that might set off a bulimic episode. This happens to severely deprived patients when they start to eat: the feeling of losing control and gobbling everything in sight and secret eating followed by purging. Purging with bulimic individuals must be monitored but not too obviously. The planning of meals should be guided by the nutritionist. Gaining patient trust is paramount and food options should reflect the likes and dislikes of the person involved. If they like meat (most don't), it should be small portions. Larger portions of vegetables and grains but beware of bulk eating, binging obscene amounts of raw veggies to fill up. Retraining eating by the nutritionist is as vital as psychotherapy and it's important to be working with a team that includes a medical doctor, psychiatrist and nutritionist.

About the Author
Janet Gilmore

Janet Gilmore was a lifelong resident of East Grand Rapids, MI. She was the daughter of Wilheimina Small and Dr. Carl Sigtenhorst. Janet was a talented artist who enjoyed painting and sculpting. She helped design and build three of her family's homes in the 1960's-1970's. She attended the University of Michigan after graduating East Grand Rapids High School in 1950. She completed a B.S. in Environmental Studies at Aquinas College in 1976.

A loving free spirit, skier, swimmer, rock and roller, Basset-lover, MG-car enthusiast, superb cook, rule-breaker and so much more. She is deeply missed but may her suffering and expression find purpose as a helping and healing voice.

Illustrated by Emma Gilmore

Emma Gilmore lives with her family in Bellingham, WA. She has been creating art from the moment she picked up her first crayon. She began illustrating interpretations of her Grandmother's poetry at age 15.

Emma is currently a high school Senior with interests in pursuing a college education and a possible career in psychology. She loves to travel, paint, listen to music, play her violin and run.

Arranged & Edited by Brian Gilmore

Brian Gilmore arranged and edited KOANS from the collection of his mother's poetry, letters, and journal. Brian lives in Bellingham, WA with his family. He is a school counselor and filmmaker.

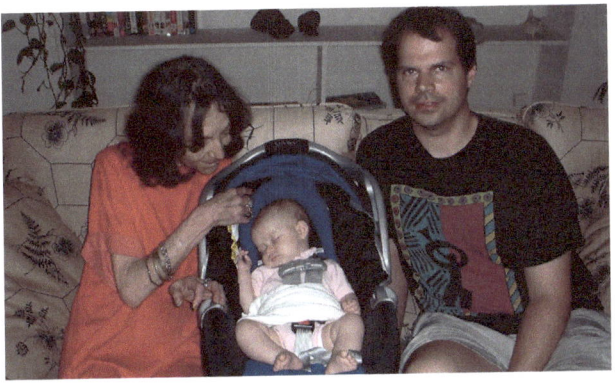

Janet, Emma & Brian (2002)

Acknowledgments

On behalf of Janet, Emma and myself, we give our heartfelt thanks to all who have supported us with this important project. Thank you Lauren Fritzen for taking the time and care to proof the Foreword and Afterword and provide your valued edits to strengthen the expression of our story. Thanks to our wonderful independent bookstore here in Bellingham, WA, Village Books, for guiding us through our first self-publication and making this loving tribute and testimony a reality.

The generosity and support from our 42 crowdfunding campaign backers was amazing. These donations provided the income to cover all of our publishing costs which allows us to donate all future profits from book sales to nonprofits serving mental health wellness. We are honored to recognize the following donors who made a contribution at our Acknowledgement Level: Dave Bird, Jim Braun, Greg Gilmore, Kristina Gilmore, Christopher Hill, David Laws, Roger and Renee Laws, Peter Leibold, The LePine Family, Jeanne Schmidt and Doug Vahey.

Also, we were so fortunate to have found an amazing group of individuals to voice Janet's words for our audio production. This could not have been possible without the generous support and talent of Anneliese Floyd, Rachel Gleason and Rachael Steil. Also, thanks to Michael Crittenden, owner of Mackinaw Harvest Studios and friend, for recording and engineering our voices during that magical session in the Fall of '18.

Finally, thanks to Randy Herman, talented musician and dear lifelong friend of mine, who my mom loved dearly, for the gift of your music for this project.

INFORMATION AND SUPPORT FOR EATING DISORDERS

Dear Reader, we can't thank you enough for your time to listen to Janet's story. If you or someone you know is struggling with an eating disorder, please seek professional help for support. A great resource to learn more is the National Eating Disorders Association.

Their website is: nationaleatingdisorders.org/help-support and their Call Helpline is (800) 931-2237.

Please note that all profits from the sale of this book will be donated to The Diatribe, an amazing nonprofit doing powerful work in West Michigan where Janet spent her entire life. The Diatribe uses performing arts to empower young people to share their stories, raise awareness of social issues, and create change within their communities.

For more information please check out their website: https://thediatribe.org

www.ingramcontent.com/pod-product-compliance
Lightning Source LLC
Chambersburg PA
CBHW041353290426

44108CB00006B/136